SYMBOLON
THE CATHOLIC FAITH EXPLAINED

Part 2
Living the Faith

Participant's Guide

Sessions 1-10

Edward Sri
Lucas Pollice
General Editors

Nihil obstat: Ben Akers, S.T.L.
Imprimatur: Most Reverend Samuel J. Aquila, S.T.L., Archbishop of Denver
June 1, 2014

Copyright © 2014/2016 Augustine Institute. All rights reserved.
With the exception of short excerpts used in articles and critical reviews, no part of this work may be reproduced, transmitted, or stored in any form whatsoever, printed or electronic, without the prior permission of the publisher.

Excerpts from the Lectionary for Mass for Use in the Dioceses of the United States of America, second typical edition © 2001, 1998, 1997, 1986, 1970 Confraternity of Christian Doctrine, Inc., Washington, D.C. Used with permission. All rights reserved. No portion of this text may be reproduced by any means without permission in writing from the copyright owner.

Some Scripture verses contained herein are from the Catholic Edition of the Revised Standard Version of the Bible, copyright ©1965, 1966 by the Division of Christian Educators of the National Council of the Churches of Christ in the United States of America. Used by permission. All rights reserved.

English translation of the *Catechism of the Catholic Church* for the United States of America, copyright ©1994, United States Catholic Conference, Inc.—Libreria Editrice Vaticana. English translation of the *Catechism of the Catholic Church*: Modification from the Editio Typica copyright ©1997, United States Catholic Conference, Inc.—Libreria Editrice Vaticana.

Writers: Woodeene Koenig-Bricker, Lucas Pollice, Edward Sri, Sean Dalton

Media/Print Production: Brenda Kraft, Justin Leddick, Kevin Mallory, John Schmidt

Graphic Design: Stacy Innerst, Jane Myers

ACKNOWLEDGMENT

We would like to acknowledge with heartfelt gratitude the many catechists, teachers, and diocesan leaders from across the country that have given invaluable advice and guidance in the development of *Symbolon*:

Michael Andrews, Keith Borchers, Steve Bozza, Dr. Chris Burgwald, James Cavanagh, Chris Chapman, Fr. Dennis Gill, Jim Gontis, Dr. Tim Gray, Lisa Gulino, Mary Hanbury, Deacon Ray Helgeson, Dr. Sean Innerst, Ann Lankford, Deacon Kurt Lucas, Sean Martin, Martha Tonn, Kyle Neilson, Michelle Nilsson, Ken Ogorek, Dr. Claude Sasso, Scott Sollom, Deacon Jim Tighe, Mary Ann Wiesinger, and Gloria Zapiain.

Augustine Institute
6160 South Syracuse Way, Suite 310
Greenwood Village, CO 80111
Information: 303-937-4420
AugustineInstitute.org

Printed in the United States of America
ISBN 978-0-9972037-5-2

SYMBOLON TABLE OF CONTENTS

SESSION 1
THE SACRAMENTS: Baptism & Confirmation 7

SESSION 2
THE EUCHARIST: Source & Summit of Christian Life 13

SESSION 3
WALK THROUGH THE MASS: Exploring the Sacred Liturgy 19

SESSION 4
PENANCE AND ANOINTING OF THE SICK: God's Mercy Revealed 25

SESSION 5
MATRIMONY AND HOLY ORDERS: The Sacraments of Service & Communion 33

SESSION 6
A CATHOLIC MORAL VISION: Virtue, Grace, & the Path to Happiness 39

SESSION 7
A LOVE THAT LASTS: Discovering Authentic Love 45

SESSION 8
A LOVE THAT LASTS: God's Plan for Sexuality 51

SESSION 9
CATHOLIC SOCIAL TEACHING: Building a Civilization of Love 57

SESSION 10
CATHOLIC SOCIAL TEACHING: Protecting the Dignity of the Human Person 65

What does *Symbolon* mean?

In the early Church, Christians described their Creed, their summary statement of faith, as the *symbolon*, the "seal" or "symbol of the faith."

In the ancient world, the Greek word *symbolon* typically described an object like a piece of parchment, a seal, or a coin that was cut in half and given to two parties. It served as a means of recognition and confirmed a relationship between the two. When the halves of the *symbolon* were reassembled, the owner's identity was verified and the relationship confirmed.

In like manner, the Creed served as a means of Christian recognition. Someone who confessed the Creed could be identified as a true Christian. Moreover, they were assured that what they professed in the Creed brought them in unity with the faith the Apostles originally proclaimed.

This series is called *Symbolon* because it intends to help bring people deeper into that communion of apostolic faith that has existed for 2,000 years in the Church that Christ founded.

AN INTRODUCTION TO SYMBOLON

Welcome to Symbolon. In *Symbolon—Knowing the Faith* (Sessions 1-10), we walked through the "big picture" of the Catholic Faith using the Creed as our guide. Now in *Symbolon—Living the Faith* (Sessions 1-10), we turn our attention to how we encounter God in the sacraments and the moral life. Through the sacraments, Christ's work of salvation is communicated to our lives. Transformed by sacramental grace, we are made capable of living a life worthy of the Gospel in imitation of Jesus Christ.

The Leader's Guide, Participant's Guide, and videos are the three components you'll be using for each of the *Symbolon* sessions. All three work together to enable the facilitator, small group leader, or catechist to help the participants to receive the Catholic Faith and apply it to their everyday lives.

PARTICIPATING IN A SYMBOLON SESSION

Everything you need to participate in a *Symbolon* session is provided for you. Your Participant's Guide and other resources are carefully crafted to lead you through an opening of your heart and mind to God's Word, into the key truths of the particular doctrine that is the focus of the session, and ultimately to make a response of faith by turning more fully to the Lord with each session.

Your Participant's Guide will take you through the steps of the session and provide plenty of space for you to take notes and make reflections for later consideration.

A typical *Symbolon* session consists of:

- **Opening Prayer:** The session opens with a prayer drawn from the rich tradition of the Church and writings of the saints. You can read along during the prayer and refer back to it during the week.

- **Introduction:** Your leader will give a brief overview of the topic, including the key points for the session. This helps you see the "big picture" of the topic and its relevance for your daily life.

- **Video Part I:** The first video introduces the topic and helps establish its relevance as you seek to deepen your relationship with God and his Church.

- **Proclamation:** Your leader might give a brief summary statement of the doctrine that is the focus of the session. It is a statement of faith in what God has revealed and an overview of the doctrine you will be learning about in more detail in the rest of the video.

- **Video Part II:** Episodes 1–6 include a second video that goes into more depth on the topic and gives a brief but thorough explanation of the essential truths that can unlock your understanding of the Church's teaching. It also includes a section on life application, calling you to a deeper conversion and inviting you to give your life more to Jesus within a particular aspect of the faith. Episodes 7–10 each cover all the necessary material in one video.

- **Life Application:** After the video, you will have a chance to reflect on discussion questions designed to help you more deeply understand and explore the key points of the session. In addition, the "Call to Conversion" will help apply what you have learned to your daily life through prayer and reflection on key verses from Scripture, Church teachings, and practical personal reflection questions.

- **Closing Prayer:** Each session concludes with a prayer that reflects fundamental teachings and helps you to focus more deeply on the truths that were revealed.

In addition, your Participant's Guide contains references and resources for further reading and study. You are encouraged to memorize and reflect on a Scripture Verse of the Week that is included with every session. These bonus materials will help you nurture the grace and faith that has been poured out through your catechetical session.

Symbolon is your guide to the depth and breadth of the Catholic Faith. By bearing witness to the beauty of the teachings and the Tradition of the Catholic Church, *Symbolon* enables you to grow in knowledge of the Catholic Faith and in relationship with our Lord along with others in your community. Through this comprehensive program, we hope God's truth and grace will transform your life.

NOTES

Session 1

THE SACRAMENTS
BAPTISM & CONFIRMATION

THE SACRAMENTS
Baptism & Confirmation

INTRODUCTION

In the Catholic Church, there are seven sacraments that are part of a Christian's spiritual life from birth to death. They are signs of grace instituted by Christ to give his divine life to us through the work of the Holy Spirit.

But what are these sacraments? Why are they necessary for a relationship with Jesus? And how do the sacraments affect our lives on a daily basis?

These are some of the questions we will be talking about this week. We will be looking at the seven sacraments recognized by the Catholic Church in general, and then we will focus more specifically on two Sacraments of Initiation: Baptism and Confirmation. Along the way, we will see how the sacraments are part of our "toolkit" as we grow and mature in our faith and our relationship with the Church.

THIS SESSION WILL COVER:

- **What is a sacrament?**
- **The different kinds of sacraments**
- **How the sacraments are a key part of the Christian life**
- **Why Baptism is considered the "gateway" to the Christian life**
- **Why Catholics baptize infants**
- **The significance of Confirmation and its relationship to Baptism**

Cover Photo Credit: Baptism of the Lord © Zvonimir Atletic/Shutterstock.com

Session 1 THE SACRAMENTS

🕯 OPENING PRAYER

Praise the Lord!
I will give thanks to the Lord with my whole heart,
in the company of the upright, in the congregation.
Great are the works of the Lord,
studied by all who have pleasure in them.
Full of honor and majesty is his work,
and his righteousness endures for ever.
He has caused his wonderful works to be remembered;
the Lord is gracious and merciful.
He provides food for those who fear him;
he is ever mindful of his covenant.
He has shown his people the power of his works,
in giving them the heritage of the nations.
The works of his hands are faithful and just;
all his precepts are trustworthy,
they are established for ever and ever,
to be performed with faithfulness and uprightness.
He sent redemption to his people;
he has commanded his covenant for ever.
Holy and awesome is his name!
The fear of the Lord is the beginning of wisdom;
a good understanding have all those who practice it.
His praise endures for ever!   —Psalm 111

> *"These three things God requires of all the Baptized: right faith in the heart, truth on the tongue, temperance in the body."*
> —St. Gregory Nazianzen

❓ DISCUSSION QUESTIONS

1. How would you respond to someone who asks: "Why have you Catholics made Christianity so complicated with all your rules and rituals?"

2. In the video, the presenters said that the sacraments are divided into three groups. What are the three groups, and which sacraments are in each group?

3. Why is it significant that in Confirmation we are anointed with Sacred Chrism?

Session 1 THE SACRAMENTS

CALL TO CONVERSION

After spending a few moments in prayer, write down your thoughts and reflections on the following questions:

#1 In the video, we are told that the sacraments are "our toolkit as we step out every day as a believer." What does this mean to you? How can Baptism be a tool for daily life? If you have been baptized, what does this mean to you? If you are anticipating Baptism, what are you looking forward to? In what other ways can the sacraments, especially the Eucharist, become your "toolkit" for your spiritual life?

_____
_____
_____
_____

#2 Consider the following quote from St. Diadochos of Photiki:

"Before holy baptism, grace encourages the soul towards good from the outside, while Satan lurks in its depths, trying to block all the intellect's ways of approach to the divine. But from the moment that we are reborn through baptism, the demon is outside, grace is within. Thus, whereas before baptism error ruled the soul, after baptism truth rules it."

What does it mean that after Baptism "grace is within"? How does the knowledge that through Baptism you have the power and the ability to resist temptation affect you? If you truly acted as if you knew you had that power, how would your life be different from now on?

_____
_____
_____
_____

Photo Credit: Blessed Sacraments on the Altar © Alis Leonte/Shutterstock.com

#3 In the video, we heard that the sacraments fill us with Christ's life and draw us deeper into communion with God. When we want to grow spiritually or morally, we need to go to the sacraments where Jesus waits to heal, sanctify, and restore us. The presenter then asked questions that we must all answer: Will you make it a priority to frequent the sacraments? Are you willing to make the sacraments an essential part of your life? How can you begin to encounter Christ in the frequent reception of the sacraments, especially the Eucharist, and make this encounter a main emphasis in your life?

_____
_____
_____

CLOSING PRAYER

Renewal of Baptismal Promises
(If you have not yet been baptized, silently reflect on these words and the Christian life you may soon be entering.)

V. Do you reject Satan?
R. I do.
V. And all his works?
R. I do.
V. And all his empty promises?
R. I do.
V. Do you believe in God, the Father Almighty, creator of heaven and earth?
R. I do.
V. Do you believe in Jesus Christ, his only Son, our Lord, who was born of the Virgin Mary, was crucified, died, and was buried, rose from the dead, and is now seated at the right hand of the Father?
R. I do.
V. Do you believe in the Holy Spirit, the holy Catholic Church, the communion of saints, the forgiveness of sins, the resurrection of the body, and life everlasting?
R. I do.
V. God, the all-powerful Father of our Lord Jesus Christ, has given us a new birth by water and the Holy Spirit, and forgiven all our sins. May he also keep us faithful to our Lord Jesus Christ forever and ever.
R. Amen.

Session 1 THE SACRAMENTS

SCRIPTURE VERSE FOR THE WEEK

Here is a verse from the Bible that you can memorize and reflect on this week to help you apply today's session to your daily life:

 "For in one Spirit we were all baptized into one body—Jews or Greeks, slaves or free—and all were made to drink of one Spirit."
—1 Corinthians 12:13

DO YOU WANT TO MAKE THE SACRAMENTS AN IMPORTANT PART OF YOUR LIFE?

TO ENRICH YOUR CATHOLIC FAITH, VISIT formed.org

Where you'll find helpful videos, audio presentations, ebooks, and feature films from the most trustworthy presenters in the Catholic world.

For Further Reading:

For more in-depth reading about the sacraments, see the following *Catechism* passages:

- *The Sacraments: CCC 1210–1211*
- *Baptism: CCC 1214–1284*
- *Confirmation: CCC 1285–1321*

Other Resources:

- *The United States Catechism for Adults,* **Chapters 15–16**
- *Sacraments in Scripture* **by Tim Gray**
- *Living the Sacraments: Grace into Action* **by Bert Ghezzi**
- *Swear to God: The Promise and Power of the Sacraments* **by Scott Hahn**

Session 2

THE EUCHARIST
SOURCE & SUMMIT OF CHRISTIAN LIFE

Session **2** THE EUCHARIST

THE EUCHARIST
Source & Summit of Christian Life

INTRODUCTION

It has been said that the Eucharist is not a "what," but a "who."

At the very center of the Catholic Faith is the belief that the Eucharist is not merely a symbol or reminder of Jesus. No, the Eucharist is much more than that. At Mass, the bread and wine on the altar are actually changed into the very Body and Blood of Jesus. When we receive the Eucharist, therefore, we are united with Jesus himself in the most intimate way possible here on earth. The almighty God, Creator of the universe, humbles himself so that he can become one with each of us. God is within us, within our very souls, each time we attend Mass and receive Communion. What an amazing gift the Eucharist is!

But how can this be? Is Jesus really present in the Eucharist? Is the Eucharist *really* a "who"—the Real Presence of Jesus among us? The Eucharist at Mass doesn't look like flesh and blood. The Eucharist looks like bread and wine—how can Catholicism claim that it's Jesus's Body and Blood? These are some of the questions we will consider in this week's session.

THIS SESSION WILL COVER:

- **The Eucharist as Real Presence—what it means and why it is central to the Catholic Faith**
- **Why Jesus couldn't have been speaking metaphorically when he said to eat his Body and drink his Blood**
- **The Eucharist as sacrifice—how the sacrifice of the Mass makes present Christ's sacrifice on the Cross, and how knowing this makes a crucial difference for our participation in the Mass**
- **The Eucharist as Communion—how Jesus longs for us to receive him in Holy Communion**
- **How Christ's Eucharistic presence remains with us in the tabernacles in our Catholic churches, where the consecrated hosts are kept**

Cover Photo Credit: The Last Supper Juan De Juanes/shutterstock.com

Session 2 THE EUCHARIST

🕯 OPENING PRAYER

Soul of Christ, be my sanctification;
Body of Christ, be my salvation;
Blood of Christ, fill all my veins;
Water of Christ's side, wash out my stains;
Passion of Christ, my comfort be;
O good Jesus, listen to me;
In Thy wounds I fain would hide;
Ne'er to be parted from Thy side;
Guard me, should the foe assail me;
Call me when my life shall fail me;
Bid me come to Thee above,
With Thy saints to sing Thy love,
World without end. Amen.
—Prayer known as the *Anima Christi*

> *"This food is known among us as the Eucharist. We do not receive these things as common bread and common drink but as Jesus Christ, our Savior, being made flesh by the word of God."*
> —St. Justin Martyr, 2nd century

❓ DISCUSSION QUESTIONS

1. St. Thomas Aquinas wrote in a beautiful Eucharistic hymn: "Faith will tell us Christ is present, when our human senses fail." What does this mean to you?

2. What is the relationship between the Eucharist and the Jewish feast of Passover? How might the Passover background shed light on the need to receive Jesus in Holy Communion? How might the Passover background shed light on the Mass as sacrifice?

3. How can the Eucharist be a true sacrifice when Jesus is no longer dying on the Cross, but has been raised from the dead and is seated in Heaven?

Session **2** THE EUCHARIST

CALL TO CONVERSION

After spending a few moments in prayer, write down your thoughts and reflections on the following questions:

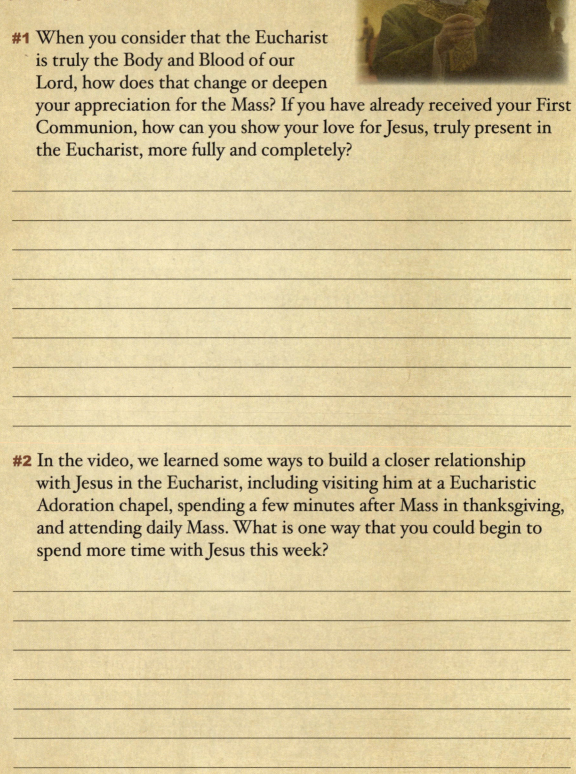

#1 When you consider that the Eucharist is truly the Body and Blood of our Lord, how does that change or deepen your appreciation for the Mass? If you have already received your First Communion, how can you show your love for Jesus, truly present in the Eucharist, more fully and completely?

___

#2 In the video, we learned some ways to build a closer relationship with Jesus in the Eucharist, including visiting him at a Eucharistic Adoration chapel, spending a few minutes after Mass in thanksgiving, and attending daily Mass. What is one way that you could begin to spend more time with Jesus this week?

___

Photo Credit: Communion with Father John © 2014 AugustineInstitute.org

Session 2 THE EUCHARIST

#3 Reflect on the following quote from St. Thérèse of Lisieux:

"Do you realize that Jesus is there in the tabernacle expressly for you—for you alone? He burns with the desire to come into your heart…go without fear to receive the Jesus of peace and love."

When you read that Jesus is waiting for you alone, what thoughts come to mind? How can you best respond to this invitation of love? What fears or concerns are holding you back? Can you let them go and "receive the Jesus of peace and love"?

_____
_____
_____
_____
_____
_____
_____

CLOSING PRAYER

May the partaking of your Holy Mysteries, O Lord,
be not for my judgment or condemnation,
but for the healing of soul and body.
O Lord, I also believe and profess
that this (which I am about to receive)
is truly your most precious Body
and your life-giving Blood,
which, I pray, make me worthy to receive
for the remission of all my sins
and for life everlasting. Amen.

—Prayer before Holy Communion
from the Byzatine Liturgy

Photo Credit: Mosaic-Last Supper-Bremen Cathedral © Hadrian/Shutterstock.com

Session 2 THE EUCHARIST

SCRIPTURE VERSE FOR THE WEEK

Here is a verse from the Bible that you can memorize and reflect on this week to help you apply today's session to your daily life:

"For as often as you eat this bread and drink the cup, you proclaim the Lord's death until he comes."
—I Corinthians 11:26

MEET JESUS IN THE EUCHARIST!

TO ENRICH YOUR CATHOLIC FAITH, VISIT formed.org

Where you'll find helpful videos, audio presentations, ebooks, and feature films from the most trustworthy presenters in the Catholic world.

For Further Reading:

For more in-depth reading about the Eucharist, see the following *Catechism* passages:

- *The Names of the Sacrament:* CCC 1328–1332
- *Bread and Wine; Body and Blood:* CCC 1333
- *Institution of the Eucharist:* CCC 1337–1344
- *Sacramental Sacrifice:* CCC 1357–1368
- *Transubstantiation:* CCC 1376–1377
- *Fruits of Communion:* CCC 1391–1395

Other Resources:

- *The United States Catechism for Adults,* Chapter 17
- *St. John Paul II, Encyclical Letter Ecclesia de Eucharistia (On the Eucharist in its Relationship to the Church)*
- *The Eucharist: A Bible Study Guide for Catholics* by Fr. Mitch Pacwa
- *Jesus and the Jewish Roots of the Eucharist: Unlocking the Secrets of the Last Supper* by Brant Pitre
- *God Is Near Us: the Eucharist, the Heart of Life* by Joseph Cardinal Ratzinger
- *Code of Canon Law,* 912–923 (available at www.vatican.va)

Session 3

WALK THROUGH THE MASS
EXPLORING THE SACRED LITURGY

Session **3** WALK THROUGH THE MASS

WALK THROUGH THE MASS
Exploring the Sacred Liturgy

INTRODUCTION

One of the things that makes the Roman Catholic Mass unique is that no matter where in the world you go, the Mass will be the same. Of course, the language may be different and so may the music and decorations, but the essence will be the same from Australia to Zimbabwe. Every Mass will have the Scripture readings and the consecration of the bread and wine. It's one reason why it is "Catholic"—the very word means "universal," and the Mass is indeed universal.

The sacred rites that make up the Mass come to us directly from the days of the Apostles. In Acts and the Epistles, we read how believers gathered on the Lord's Day to celebrate the Lord's Supper. Readings from Scripture, a homily, prayers of petition, and the offering of bread and wine were key aspects of the Mass then, just as they are today.

In the Holy Sacrifice of the Mass, we participate in the one sacrifice of Jesus at Calvary. In order to understand what is happening, in this session we will look at how the Mass is constructed and what happens in the two major parts: the Liturgy of the Word and the Liturgy of the Eucharist. We will see how, when we participate in Mass, we truly enter into the most profound union possible with God.

THIS SESSION WILL COVER:

- **How the Mass we celebrate today links back to apostolic times**
- **The four main sections of the Mass**
- **How we encounter God in the Liturgy of the Word and the Liturgy of the Eucharist**
- **What we can do to "get more" out of every Mass**
- **Why we must attend Mass on Sundays and Holy Days of Obligation**

Cover Photo Credit: The Mass for the Foundation of the Order of the Trinitarians/Scala/Art Resource, NY

Session 3 WALK THROUGH THE MASS

OPENING PRAYER

Almighty and everlasting God,
behold I come to the Sacrament
of thine only-begotten Son,
our Lord Jesus Christ:
I come as one infirm to the physician of life,
as one unclean to the fountain of mercy,
as one blind to the light of everlasting brightness,
as one poor and needy to the Lord of heaven and earth.
Therefore I implore the abundance of thy measureless bounty
that thou wouldst vouchsafe to heal my infirmity,
wash my uncleanness,
enlighten my blindness,
enrich my poverty
and clothe my nakedness,
that I may receive the Bread of Angels,
the King of kings, the Lord of lords,
with such reverence and humility,
with such sorrow and devotion,
with such purity and faith,
with such purpose and intention
as may be profitable to my soul's salvation.
Amen.
— From the Prayer before Mass by St. Thomas Aquinas

> *"The celebration of Holy Mass is as valuable as the death of Jesus on the cross."*
> —St. Thomas Aquinas

DISCUSSION QUESTIONS

1. What are some examples of words in the Mass that come directly from Scripture? What are some examples that come from the earliest days of the Church?

2. In the video presentation, we learned that in the Mass, Christ's sacrifice is made present. In what ways are we called to unite our lives to Christ's sacrifice made present in the Mass?

3. What would you say to a friend who says it is not necessary to attend Mass every Sunday?

Session 3 WALK THROUGH THE MASS

CALL TO CONVERSION

After spending a few moments in prayer, write down your thoughts and reflections on the following questions:

#1 Do I come to Mass to receive or to give? What am I doing to prepare my soul for Mass?

_____
_____
_____
_____
_____
_____
_____
_____
_____
_____

#2 In the video, we learned some ways to "get more out of the Mass," including praying in the car on the way to church, listening for a specific point or prayer that particularly touches us, and remaining for a few minutes after Mass to give thanks. What is one thing that you could do this week to prepare for Mass?

_____
_____
_____
_____
_____
_____
_____
_____
_____
_____

Photo Credit: The Mass for the Foundation of the Order of the Trinitarians/Scala/Art Resource, NY

Session 3 WALK THROUGH THE MASS

#3 Reflect on the following quote from St. Padre Pio of Pietrelcina:

"It would be easier for the world to survive without the sun than to do without Holy Mass."

Prayerfully consider how St. Padre Pio's statement expresses the importance of the Mass. How does this change the way you view the obligation to attend Mass? How can you more completely give yourself to Jesus at each Mass?

_____
_____
_____
_____
_____
_____

CLOSING PRAYER

I give thanks to thee, O Lord,
most holy, Father almighty, eternal God,
that thou hast vouchsafed,
for no merit of mine own,
but out of thy pure mercy,
to appease the hunger
of my soul with the precious
body and blood of thy Son,
Our Lord Jesus Christ.
Humbly I implore thee,
let not this Holy Communion
be to me an increase of guilt
unto my punishment,
but an availing plea unto pardon
and salvation.
Amen.
— From the Prayer after Mass
by St. Thomas Aquinas

Photo Credit: St. Joseph Church Mass © 2013 Brenda Kraft/AugustineInstitute.org

SCRIPTURE VERSE FOR THE WEEK

Here is a verse from the Bible that you can memorize and reflect on this week to help you apply today's session to your daily life:

 "Truly, truly, I say to you, unless you eat the flesh of the Son of Man and drink his blood, you have no life in you." —John 6:53

DO YOU WANT TO FURTHER EXPLORE THE MASS?

TO ENRICH YOUR CATHOLIC FAITH, VISIT formed.org

Where you'll find helpful videos, audio presentations, ebooks, and feature films from the most trustworthy presenters in the Catholic world.

For Further Reading:

For more in-depth reading about the Mass, see the following *Catechism* passages:

- *The Mass through the Ages:* **CCC 1345**
- *The Structure of the Mass:* **CCC 1346**
- *Introductory Rites:* **CCC 1348**
- *The Liturgy of the Word:* **CCC 1349**
- *The Offertory:* **CCC 1350**
- *The Liturgy of the Eucharist:* **CCC 1351–1353**
- *Sunday Obligation:* **CCC 1389, 1417**

Other Resources:

- *The United States Catechism for Adults,* **Chapter 14**
- *A Biblical Walk through the Mass: Understanding What We Say and Do in the Liturgy* **by Dr. Edward Sri**
- *The Mass: The Glory, the Mystery, the Tradition* **by Cardinal Donald Wuerl and Mike Aquilina**
- *The Mass of the Early Christians* **by Mike Aquilina**
- *The Lamb's Supper: The Mass as Heaven on Earth* **by Scott Hahn**

Session 4

PENANCE AND ANOINTING OF THE SICK

GOD'S MERCY REVEALED

Session **4** PENANCE AND ANOINTING OF THE SICK

PENANCE AND ANOINTING OF THE SICK
God's Mercy Revealed

INTRODUCTION

We are all in need of healing. Some of us may need physical or emotional healing, but all of us need spiritual healing. St. Paul says in Romans 3:23, "All have sinned and fall short of the glory of God."

God knows that we cannot make amends for our sins on our own. That is the fundamental reason that he sent Jesus—to save us from our sins. But in our everyday life, we often "fall short." For that reason, God has provided us with two sacraments designed especially for healing: the Sacrament of Penance and the Sacrament of the Anointing of the Sick.

In the Sacrament of Penance, we obtain God's pardon for our sins, and, at the same time, we are reconciled to the Church and God's people. Through this sacrament, we receive the spiritual healing we all need.

At times, however, we may also benefit from the second sacrament of healing—the Anointing of the Sick. In this sacrament, a baptized person who is in danger of death because of illness or old age receives strength, courage, and peace to endure their suffering, and the forgiveness of sins if the person is not able to receive the Sacrament of Penance. The sacrament also can bring restoration of health, if it is conducive to the person's salvation, and it prepares them for passing to eternal life.

THIS SESSION WILL COVER:

- Why Penance is such an important part of the Catholic Faith
- Why we confess our sins to a priest
- A step-by-step guide to the reception of the Sacrament of Penance
- The benefits and graces of frequent Confession
- And finally, a look at the other sacrament of healing— The Anointing of the Sick

Cover Photo Credit: The prodigal son by Murillo. © Restored Traditions. Used by permission.

Session 4 PENANCE AND ANOINTING OF THE SICK

OPENING PRAYER

Lord, you invite all who are burdened to come to you.
Allow your healing hand to heal me.
Touch my soul with your compassion for others.
Touch my heart with your
courage and infinite love for all.
Touch my mind with your wisdom,
that my mouth may always
proclaim your praise.
Teach me to reach out to
you in my need,
and help me to lead others to
you by my example.
Most loving heart of Jesus,
bring me health in body and spirit
that I may serve you with
all my strength.
Touch gently this life
which you have created, now and forever. Amen.

—www.ourcatholicfaith.org

"But if a person, whether a layperson, priest or sister, goes to confession and converts, the Lord forgives. And when the Lord forgives, he forgets."

—Pope Francis

DISCUSSION QUESTIONS

1. How can we keep our eyes fixed on Jesus so that we are not susceptible to sin?

2. According to the presenters, what are the effects of the Sacrament of Penance?

3. What is keeping you from encountering Jesus in the Sacrament of Penance more often?

Photo Credit: Church at Serralunga D'Alba, Northern Italy © Rostislav Glinsky/Shutterstock.com

Session **4** PENANCE AND ANOINTING OF THE SICK

CALL TO CONVERSION

After spending a few moments in prayer, write down your thoughts and reflections on the following questions:

#1 Recall the Gospel story of the woman caught in adultery and the story of the prodigal son. What do these stories reveal about God's mercy and his desire to forgive and heal you?

_____
_____
_____
_____

#2 Read and reflect on the following message from Pope Francis to the General Audience at St. Peter's Square (2/19/14):

"One might say: I confess only to God. Yes, you can say to God 'forgive me' and say your sins, but our sins are also committed against the brethren, and against the Church. That is why it is necessary to ask pardon of the Church, and of the brethren in the person of the priest. 'But Father, I am ashamed ....' Shame is also good, it is healthy to feel a little shame, because being ashamed is salutary. When a person feels no shame, in my country we say that he is 'shameless'; 'sin vergüenza.' But shame too does good, because it makes us more humble, and the priest receives this confession with love and tenderness and forgives us on God's behalf. Also from a human point of view, in order to unburden oneself, it is good to talk with a brother and tell the priest these things which are weighing so much on my heart. And one feels that one is unburdening oneself before God, with the Church, with his brother. Do not be afraid of Confession! When one is in line to go to Confession, one feels all these things, even shame, but then when one finishes Confession one leaves free, grand, beautiful, forgiven, candid, happy. This is the beauty of Confession!"

#3 What is keeping you from encountering Jesus in the Sacrament of Penance? Is there something that you need to confess in order to be "restored to health"? Remember what Pope St. John Paul II said:

"Confession is an act of honesty and courage—an act of entrusting ourselves, beyond sin, to the mercy of a loving and forgiving God."

_____
_____
_____
_____

Session 4 — PENANCE AND ANOINTING OF THE SICK

Examination of Conscience Based on the Ten Commandments

1. I am the Lord your God. You shall have no false gods before me.

Do I put God before my spouse? My children? My work?
Do I believe that God loves me?
Do I have any "false gods" in my life like money, fame, power, or possessions?
Have I been involved in fortune-telling, astrology, palm-reading or witchcraft?
Do I pray daily?

2. You shall not take the name of the Lord your God in vain.

Do I use curse words?
Have I made oaths or sworn promises to God that I haven't kept?
Have I allowed others to swear in my presence?

3. Remember to keep holy the Lord's Day.

Do I attend Mass on Sundays and Holy Days of Obligation?
Do I avoid unnecessary work on Sundays?
Do I avoid unnecessary shopping on Sundays?

4. Honor your father and mother.

Do I show love to my parents, regardless of their age?
Do I help them when I can?
Do I respect my employer and others in authority?
If I am a parent, have I given a bad example in word or deed to my children?
Am I raising my children in the Catholic Faith?

5. You shall not kill.

Have I killed or seriously injured anyone?
Do I gossip?
Have I had an abortion or helped someone get an abortion?
Have I lost my temper, given into anger, or harbored resentment against my neighbor?
Do I bear grudges?
Have I ever harmed anyone physically, mentally or emotionally?
Do I take care of the environment?

6. You shall not commit adultery.

Have I used pornography?
Have I watched movies that are overly violent or sexual?
Have I consented to lustful thoughts?
Have I masturbated?
Have I had premarital sex?
Have I treated anyone as an object, rather than a person?
Do I eat or drink in excess?
Have I lost sobriety through drunkenness or drug use?

7. You shall not steal.

Have I stolen anything?
Do I always give a full day's work for a full day's pay?
Do I cheat in school or in business?
Am I fair in paying my employees?
Am I honest in paying my taxes?
Have I wasted time?
Have I been generous in serving the poor?

8. You shall not bear false witness against your neighbor.

Have I told a lie, even a white lie?
Have I told lies to avoid getting in trouble?
Have I revealed other people's secrets?
Have I failed to mind my own business?
Have I accused someone falsely?
Have I judged others harshly?
Have I been prejudiced or discriminated against anyone?

9. You shall not covet your neighbor's wife.

Have I been unfaithful to my spouse in either my actions or my thoughts?
Have I used my wife or husband merely to satisfy my sexual urges?
Have I acted inappropriately with those of the opposite sex?

10. You shall not covet your neighbor's property.

Have I envied anyone else's possessions, money, fame, or success?
Have I used more than my fair share of resources?

CLOSING PRAYER

Act of Contrition

O my God, I am heartily sorry for having offended thee, and I detest all my sins because of thy just punishments, but most of all because they offend thee, my God, who art all-good and deserving of all my love. I firmly resolve, with the help of thy grace, to sin no more and to avoid the near occasions of sin. Amen.

SCRIPTURE VERSE FOR THE WEEK

Here is a verse from the Bible that you can memorize and reflect on this week to help you apply today's session to your daily life:

"Blessed is he whose transgression is forgiven, whose sin is covered."
—Psalm 32:1

Photo Credit: Healing of the Demoniac © ruskpp/Shutterstock.com

Session **4** PENANCE AND ANOINTING OF THE SICK

DO YOU WANT TO LEARN MORE ABOUT PENANCE AND ANOINTING OF THE SICK?

TO ENRICH YOUR CATHOLIC FAITH, VISIT formed.org

Where you'll find helpful videos, audio presentations, ebooks, and feature films from the most trustworthy presenters in the Catholic world.

For Further Reading:

For more in-depth reading about Penance and Anointing of the Sick, see the following *Catechism* passages:

- *Jesus Reconciles Us to the Father: CCC 1485*
- *Names of the Sacrament of Penance: CCC 1423–1424*
- *God Alone Forgives Sin: CCC 1441*
- *Priests Given Power of Forgiveness: CCC 1442, 1444–1445*
- *The Spiritual Effects of the Sacrament of Penance: CCC 1496*
- *Contrition: CCC 1451*
- *Absolution: CCC 1449*
- *Anointing of the Sick: CCC 1532*

Other Resources:

- *The United States Catechism for Adults,* Chapters 18–19
- *Apostolic Exhortation, Reconcilio et Paenitentia* by Pope St. John Paul II
- *Lord, Have Mercy: The Healing Power of Confession* by Scott Hahn
- *Going to Confession?* by United States Conference of Catholic Bishops
- *Go in Peace: Your Guide to the Purpose and Power of Confession* by Father Mitch Pacwa and Sean Brown
- *The Light Is On for You: The Life-Changing Power of Confession* by Cardinal Donald Wuerl
- *Pastoral Care of the Sick (Bilingual Edition)* by United States Conference of Catholic Bishops

Session 4 — PENANCE AND ANOINTING OF THE SICK

NOTES

Session 5

MATRIMONY AND HOLY ORDERS

THE SACRAMENTS OF SERVICE & COMMUNION

MATRIMONY AND HOLY ORDERS
The Sacraments of Service & Communion

INTRODUCTION

All marriages begin with hopes and dreams, but according to Professor Scott Stanley at the University of Denver, a young couple marrying for the first time today has a lifetime divorce risk of forty percent. And of those married couples who do stay together, how many truly reflect the loving union of man and woman that God intended marriage to be?

Perhaps part of the reason so many marriages struggle is that we forget marriage is a sacrament. The wedding ceremony is a wonderful event, but the Sacrament of Matrimony doesn't end with the vows on the wedding day; it just begins then. Through the sacrament, God gives married couples the grace they need to live their call to service, sacrifice, mutual sanctification, openness to new life, and lifelong faithfulness to each other.

A strong marriage is formed day by day, over a lifetime, as a husband and wife grow in love, trust, and mutual self-giving.

None of these things are easy. But through the graces of the sacrament, those who are called to the married state are given strength to love as Christ loved—and to make their marriage a witness to God's own love for the world.

THIS SESSION WILL COVER:

- **Why marriage is a sacrament**
- **The concrete ways the sacrament helps couples every day**
- **How Christ's love for his Church is the model for marriage**
- **The importance of the lifelong commitment of marriage**
- **What an annulment is…and isn't**
- **The second sacrament of service—Holy Orders—and how this sacrament comes in an unbroken line from the Apostles**

Cover Photo Credit: Marriage of Emanuele Filiberto I of Savoy and Margaret of Valois © DeA Picture Library/Art Resource, NY

Session 5 — MATRIMONY AND HOLY ORDERS

OPENING PRAYER

God our Father, we give you thanks
for the gift of marriage: the bond of life and love,
and the font of the family.

The love of husband and wife enriches your Church with children,
fills the world with a multitude of spiritual fruitfulness and service,
and is the sign of the love of your Son, Jesus Christ, for his Church.

May your Holy Spirit enlighten our society
to treasure the heroic love of husband and wife,
and guide our leaders to sustain and protect
the singular place of mothers and fathers
in the lives of their children.

We ask all these things through Christ our Lord,
Amen.

–Prayer for the Defense of Marriage from the U.S. Catholic Bishops

> *"If two pieces of wood are carefully glued together, their union will be so close that it is easier to break them in some fresh place than where they were joined; and God so united man and wife, that it is easier to sever soul and body than those two."*
> —St. Francis de Sales

DISCUSSION QUESTIONS

1. What are the four aspects of Catholic marriage as reflected in the Sacrament of Matrimony, and what does each entail?

2. After his second divorce, a popular American entertainer had this to say about marriage in an interview on television: "Well if you have to work at it then maybe it's not worth having…I have to work at everything else in my life. I have to work at my work. I just think a marriage should be easy, not hard." How would you respond to that comment?

3. A priest said: "While it is true that no one will ever call me 'daddy,' thousands call me 'Father.'" Why do we call priests "Father"?

Session 5 MATRIMONY AND HOLY ORDERS

CALL TO CONVERSION

After spending a few moments in prayer, write down your thoughts and reflections on the following questions:

#1 If you are married, how does your union signify the union of Christ and the Church? In what areas do you fall short? Where can you improve? Are you asking God for the daily grace of the Sacrament?

_____
_____
_____
_____

#2 If you aren't married, how can you use your single state to reflect Christ's sacrificial love and service to others more?

_____
_____
_____
_____

#3 Reflect on the following quote from Pope St. John Paul II:

"Marriage is an act of will that signifies and involves a mutual gift, which unites the spouses and binds them to their eventual souls, with whom they make up a sole family—a domestic church."

How is the marriage relationship not just a feeling but an "act of the will"? How does this differ from what the world thinks about marriage?

_____
_____
_____
_____

Photo Credit: Deacon at St. Joseph Church © Brenda Kraft/AugustineInstitute.org

Session 5 MATRIMONY AND HOLY ORDERS

CLOSING PRAYER

O God, Father of all mercies,
Provider of a bountiful harvest,
send your graces upon those
you have called to gather the
fruits of your labor;
preserve and strengthen them
in their lifelong service of you.

Open the hearts of your children
that they may discern your holy will;
inspire in them a love and desire to
surrender themselves to serving others
in the name of your Son, Jesus Christ.

Teach all your faithful to follow their respective paths in life
guided by your divine Word and truth.
Through the intercession of the Most Blessed Virgin Mary,
all the angels, and saints, humbly hear our prayers
and grant your Church's needs, through Christ, our Lord.
Amen.
—U.S. Catholic Bishops' Prayer for the Discernment of Vocations

SCRIPTURE VERSE FOR THE WEEK

Here is a verse from the Bible that you can memorize and reflect on this week to help you apply today's session to your daily life:

 Therefore a man leaves his father and his mother and cleaves to his wife, and they become one flesh. —Genesis 2:24

Photo Credit: Marriage at Cana by G. David © Restored Traditions. Used by permission.

Session 5 MATRIMONY AND HOLY ORDERS

DO YOU WANT TO LEARN MORE ABOUT MARRIAGE AND HOLY ORDERS?

TO ENRICH YOUR CATHOLIC FAITH, VISIT formed.org

Where you'll find helpful videos, audio presentations, ebooks, and feature films from the most trustworthy presenters in the Catholic world.

For Further Reading:

For more in-depth reading about Matrimony and Holy Orders, see the following *Catechism* passages:

- *Marriage in God's Plan: CCC 1602–1605*
- *Marriage in the Lord: CCC 1612*
- *Marriage as a Model of Christ's Union with the Church: CCC 1616*
- *The Rites of Marriage: CCC 1621–1624*
- *Matrimonial Consent: CCC 1625–1629*
- *Mixed Marriage and Disparity of Cult: CCC 1633–1636*
- *Permanence of Marriage: CCC 1638–1640*
- *Grace of the Sacrament: CCC 1641–1642*
- *The Indissolubility of Marriage: CCC 1644*
- *Fidelity of Conjugal Love: CCC 1646*
- *Openness to Fertility: CCC 1652–1654*
- *Holy Orders: CCC 1536–1538*

Other Resources:

- *The United States Catechism for Adults,* Chapters 20–21
- *Life-Giving Love: Embracing God's Beautiful Design for Marriage* by Scott Hahn and Kimberly Hahn
- *Men, Women and the Mystery of Love: Practical Insights from John Paul II's Love and Responsibility* by Edward Sri
- *Three to Get Married* by Venerable Fulton J. Sheen
- *Marriage: The Mystery of Faithful Love* by Dietrich Von Hildebrand
- *Marriage: Love and Life in the Divine Plan* from USCCB United States Conference of Catholic Bishops
- *Apostolic Exhortation Familiaris Consortio* by Pope St. John Paul II
- *To Save a Thousand Souls* by Fr. Brett Brannen

Session 6

A CATHOLIC MORAL VISION

VIRTUE, GRACE, & THE PATH TO HAPPINESS

Session 6 A CATHOLIC MORAL VISION

A CATHOLIC MORAL VISION
Virtue, Grace, & the Path to Happiness

INTRODUCTION

The dictionary defines *morality* as "a system of ideas of right and wrong conduct." The problem today is that our culture doesn't accept that there is an absolute standard for right and wrong. Instead, much of what the world believes is based on moral relativism: the idea that there isn't really right or wrong, truth or falsehood—all that matters is what you think and feel is right. Any moral law that applies to everyone is viewed as a restriction of your freedom.

This stands in stark contrast to Catholic teaching, which says that living a moral life according to the guidance God has given us is the key to true happiness and freedom. According to Catholic thought, morality is the map that helps us build a life that allows us to become all that God has created us to be. Rather than being restrictive, morality liberates us from sin and enslavement to our own selfish desires.

We will look at God's moral vision for our lives and how by following it, we become authentically whole and holy.

THIS SESSION WILL COVER:

- **What leads to true happiness**
- **The difference between the modern view of freedom and the biblical view of freedom**
- **Virtue and why we need it to live life well**
- **The three things that make an act moral**
- **Why we can never do evil so that good may result—in other words, why the end never justifies the means**
- **Sin and how it hinders our pursuit of happiness**
- **What we need to have a correctly formed conscience**

Cover Photo Credit: The Presentation of the Tablets of Law to the Hebrews/Scala/Art Resource, NY

Session **6** A CATHOLIC MORAL VISION

OPENING PRAYER

Christ Jesus, Sweet Lord,
why have I ever loved,
why in my whole life
have I ever desired anything except you,
Jesus my God?
Where was I when I was not in spirit with you?
Now, from this time forth,
do you, all my desires, grow hot,
and flow out upon the Lord Jesus...
O, Sweet Jesus,
may every good feeling that is fitted
for your praise,
love you, delight in you, adore you!
God of my heart,
and my Portion, Christ Jesus,
may my heart faint away in spirit,
and may you be my Life within me!
—St. Augustine of Hippo

> "O my dear parishioners, let us endeavor to get to heaven! There we shall see God. How happy we shall feel! We must get to heaven! What a pity it would be if some of you were to find yourselves on the other side!"
> —St. John Vianney

DISCUSSION QUESTIONS

1. What, according to the presenter, is the hallmark of true freedom? What do we need to be truly free?

2. How do we know whether our choices are morally good? What are the three elements of a good moral act?

3. American novelist Mark Twain said: "It is curious that physical courage should be so common in the world and moral courage so rare." What is your interpretation of this quote?

CALL TO CONVERSION

After spending a few moments in prayer, write down your thoughts and reflections on the following questions:

#1 In the video, the presenters talked about how our relativistic culture says there are no moral truths for everyone to follow. Prayerfully consider some of the ways in which the relativistic culture affects you. Are you sometimes afraid or hesitant to say there are some things that are morally wrong for everyone? Are there some areas of your life where you rationalize certain immoral choices, preferring to "make up your own morality" instead of allowing the teaching of Christ and the Church to guide you?

_____
_____
_____
_____
_____

#2 Today's session discussed virtue as a habitual disposition to do the good. Prayerfully consider how well your life reflects the cardinal virtues.

a. How well do I live a prudent life, making wise decisions based on what is truly most important in life?

_____
_____
_____

b. How well do I live a temperate life, exhibiting self-control especially in attraction to pleasures of food, drink, and sex?

_____
_____
_____

Photo Credit: Archangels Michael and Gabriel © Iosif Chezan/Shutterstock.com

c. How well do I live out courage, exhibiting a consistent willingness to endure pain and suffering for what is good?

_____
_____
_____

d. How well do I exhibit justice in my daily life, fulfilling my responsibilities toward God and others in my family, friendships, workplace, and society?

_____
_____
_____

#3 Which of these virtues do you think you need to grow in most? What is one thing you can do this week to help you grow in this area? Turn to God each day in prayer, asking for his divine assistance.

_____
_____
_____
_____

CLOSING PRAYER

Our Father, who art in heaven,
hallowed be thy Name.
Thy kingdom come.
Thy will be done,
on earth as it is in heaven.
Give us this day our daily bread.
And forgive us our trespasses,
as we forgive those who
trespass against us.
And lead us not into temptation,
but deliver us from evil.
Amen.

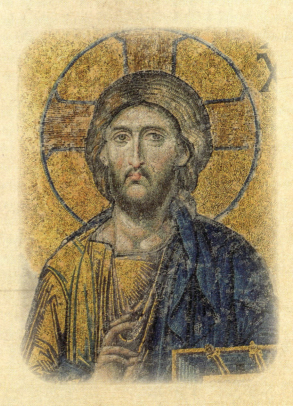

Photo Credit: Byzantine Mosaic © StefanHolm/Shutterstock.com

Session **6** A CATHOLIC MORAL VISION

SCRIPTURE VERSE FOR THE WEEK

Here is a verse from the Bible that you can memorize and reflect on this week to help you apply today's session to your daily life:

 "Turn from evil and do good; seek peace and pursue it."

—Psalm 34:14

DO YOU WANT TO LEARN MORE ABOUT THE CATHOLIC MORAL VISION?

TO ENRICH YOUR CATHOLIC FAITH, VISIT formed.org

Where you'll find helpful videos, audio presentations, ebooks, and feature films from the most trustworthy presenters in the Catholic world.

For Further Reading:

For more in-depth reading about a Catholic moral vision, see the following *Catechism* passages:

- *Freedom and Responsibility: CCC 1731–1734*
- *Freedom as a Right: CCC 1747*
- *Sources of Morality: CCC 1750–1754*
- *Good and Evil Acts: CCC 1755*
- *Formation of Conscience: CCC 1783–1785*
- *Necessity to Obey Conscience: CCC 1800*

Other Resources:

- *The United States Catechism for Adults,* Chapters 23–34
- *An Introduction to Moral Theology* by William May
- *A Refutation of Moral Relativism: Interviews with an Absolutist* by Peter Kreeft
- *Making Choices: Practical Wisdom for Everyday Moral Decisions* by Peter Kreeft
- Encyclical Letter, *Veritatis Splendor* by Pope St. John Paul II
- *The Heart of Virtue* by Donald DeMarco

Session 7

A LOVE THAT LASTS
DISCOVERING AUTHENTIC LOVE

A LOVE THAT LASTS
Discovering Authentic Love

INTRODUCTION

A Grammy-winning song asks "What's love got to do with it?" For a Catholic, the answer is everything. Love is what every human heart desires. It is, as Pope St. John Paul II says, "the fundamental and innate vocation of every human being."

So what's gone wrong with our culture, where people seek love but so often fail to find the deep, committed relationships they desire?

The problem is that all too often we focus on love that is based on passion and pleasure—love that seeks what it can get rather than what it can give—instead of the total, committed, unconditional, and sacrificial love that God has for us.

When we base our relationships on what's in it for ourselves, we are living in what is sometimes called *eros*, the passionate love that seeks pleasure in the company of a beloved. This kind of love can feel good at the beginning, but, when the tough times come, it has no lasting foundation.

Agape love, on the other hand, is the love that God has for each one of us. It is a total, committed, and unconditional love that centers not on what we can get from the other person, but on what we can give.

We may live in a culture that praises *eros*, but our hearts long for *agape*. If we are ever to find the peace and fulfillment that we all crave, we must learn how God calls us beyond *eros love* to *agape love* to make a sincere gift of ourselves, seeking the highest good of those we love, and making our own wants and needs secondary. Only then will we know true and authentic love.

Cover Photo Credit: The Happy Lovers/Erich Lessing/Art Resource, NY

Session 7 A LOVE THAT LASTS: PART I

THIS SESSION WILL COVER:

- The essential differences between *eros* and *agape*
- What it means to love according to God's plan
- Why the only way we can find the love we desire is by living God's authentic love
- The joy and freedom that comes from living *agape*—the love that lasts
- The essential characteristics of this authentic love

OPENING PRAYER

Lord, make me an instrument of thy peace;
Where there is hatred, let me sow love;
Where there is injury, pardon;
Where there is error, truth;
Where there is doubt, faith;
Where there is despair, hope;
Where there is darkness, light;
And where there is sadness, joy.
O Divine Master, grant that I may not so much seek
To be consoled as to console;
To be understood as to understand;
To be loved as to love.
For it is in giving that we receive;
It is in pardoning that we are pardoned;
And it is in dying that we are born to eternal life.
—Prayer attributed to St. Francis of Assisi

> *"Love is therefore the fundamental and innate vocation of every human being."*
> — Pope St. John Paul II

DISCUSSION QUESTIONS

1. What are some of the characteristics of *agape*? Why does *agape* fulfill us in ways that eros alone cannot?

2. How has the entertainment industry distorted the meaning of love?

3. What do you think it means that "man cannot fully find himself, except through a sincere gift of himself"?

CALL TO CONVERSION

After spending a few moments in prayer, write down your thoughts and reflections on the following questions:

#1 In the video, the presenter encourages us to prayerfully consider how the world's view of love has changed how we look at relationships. In what ways have you been influenced by the world's view of love? How might this have affected your previous (or current) relationships?

_____
_____
_____
_____
_____
_____
_____

#2 Think about what a love built on wanting the very best for another person would look like. Take some time now and reflect on how this way of loving would change your relationships with:

- Your spouse (if you have one)
- Your boyfriend/girlfriend (if you have one)
- Your children (if you have them)
- Your friends
- Your co-workers
- Your relatives

_____
_____
_____
_____
_____
_____
_____

Session 7 A LOVE THAT LASTS: PART I

#3 Reflect on the following quote from Pope Francis about *agape*.

> *"Agape, the love of each one of us for the other, from the closest to the furthest, is in fact the only way that Jesus has given us to find the way of salvation and of the Beatitudes."*

Why do you think Pope Francis says that *agape* is the "only way" to find the way of salvation? How can you live out this in your own life?

_____
_____
_____
_____
_____
_____

CLOSING PRAYER

God, my Father,
may I love you in all things and above all things.
May I reach the joy which you have prepared
for me in heaven.
Nothing is good that is against your will,
and all that is good comes from your hand.
Place in my heart a desire to please you
and fill my mind with thoughts of your love,
so that I may grow in your wisdom and
enjoy your peace.

—http://www.catholic.org/prayers

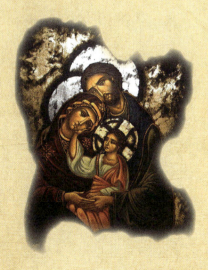

Photo Credit: The Holy Family © IOSIF CHEZAN/Shutterstock.com

Session 7 A LOVE THAT LASTS: PART I

SCRIPTURE VERSE FOR THE WEEK

Here is a verse from the Bible that you can memorize and reflect on this week to help you apply today's session to your daily life:

 So faith, hope, love abide, these three; but the greatest of these is love.
—1 Corinthians 13:13

DISCOVERING AUTHENTIC LOVE

TO ENRICH YOUR CATHOLIC FAITH, VISIT formed.org

Where you'll find helpful videos, audio presentations, ebooks, and feature films from the most trustworthy presenters in the Catholic world.

For Further Reading:

For more in-depth reading, see the following *Catechism* passages:

- *God is Love: CCC 2331*
- *Love as Vocation: CCC 2392*
- *Chastity: CCC 2337–2339*

Other Resources:

- *Marriage: Love and Life in the Divine Plan* by USCCB
- Encyclical Letter, *Deus Caritas Est* by Pope Benedict XVI
- *Men, Women and the Mystery of Love: Practical Insights from St. John Paul II's Love and Responsibility* by Edward Sri

Session 8

A LOVE THAT LASTS
GOD'S PLAN FOR SEXUALITY

Session **8** A LOVE THAT LASTS: PART II

A LOVE THAT LASTS
God's Plan for Sexuality
INTRODUCTION

God has a plan for every part of our lives—including our sexuality. The marital act is God's gift to husbands and wives, enabling them to give completely and totally of themselves to each other. In this intimate act, the couple expresses with their bodies what God means when he says two shall be one.

When a husband and wife come together, they show that God has united them in a life-long covenant of love. Sex is the way that married couples express both the physical and spiritual aspects of their love. It is the way they say, "I give myself to you totally and faithfully, holding nothing back—I give myself to you spiritually, emotionally and physically" (CCC 2360–2361).

This union of man and woman in marriage is a reflection of Christ's own love. It must be faithful, a commitment that ends only with death, and fruitful, open to the transmission of new life. The Church offers guidance that is intended to help us say "yes" to God's plan for love so that through our sexuality we can experience authentic love.

As Pope St. John Paul II said, "We are not the sum of our weaknesses and failures, we are the sum of the Father's love for us and our real capacity to become the image of His Son Jesus." The proper use of our sexuality is one way that we show the sum of that love and fulfill our capacity to become the image of Christ.

THIS SESSION WILL COVER:

- **Why sex is meant to be an expression of total, self-giving love, a love in which couples give themselves to each other physically, emotionally, and spiritually**

- **How marital sex must be both unitive and procreative**

- **How the marital embrace fits into the total, free, faithful, and fruitful aspects of marriage**

- **What the Church teaches about contraception**

- **Why the separation of pleasure from self-giving love is so destructive**

- **The challenge—and joy—of lifelong love**

Cover Photo Credit: The Garden of Eden/HIP/Art Resource, NY

Session 8 A LOVE THAT LASTS: PART II

OPENING PRAYER

Beloved, let us love one another; for love is of God, and he who loves is born of God and knows God.

He who does not love does not know God; for God is love.

In this the love of God was made manifest among us, that God sent his only Son into the world, so that we might live through him.

In this is love, not that we loved God but that he loved us and sent his Son to be the expiation for our sins.

Beloved, if God so loved us, we also ought to love one another.

No man has ever seen God; if we love one another, God abides in us and his love is perfected in us.

—I John 4:7-12

> *"Have patience with all things, but chiefly have patience with yourself. Do not lose courage in considering your own imperfections, but instantly set about remedying them—every day begin the task anew."*
> —St. Francis de Sales

DISCUSSION QUESTIONS

1. How is total and self-giving love at the very heart of our sexuality?

2. It has been said that sex is like atomic power. When used according to God's plan, it creates massive amounts of energy…but when used contrary to God's plan, it destroys. What are some examples that demonstrate this point?

3. Contraception was supposed to make marriages better, but from 1965 to 1975 the divorce rate doubled. Why do you think that is?

CALL TO CONVERSION

After spending a few moments in prayer, write down your thoughts and reflections on the following questions:

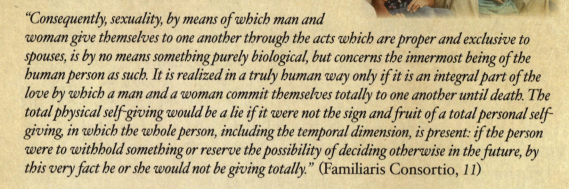

#1 Reflect on the following quote from Pope St. John Paul II:

"Consequently, sexuality, by means of which man and woman give themselves to one another through the acts which are proper and exclusive to spouses, is by no means something purely biological, but concerns the innermost being of the human person as such. It is realized in a truly human way only if it is an integral part of the love by which a man and a woman commit themselves totally to one another until death. The total physical self-giving would be a lie if it were not the sign and fruit of a total personal self-giving, in which the whole person, including the temporal dimension, is present: if the person were to withhold something or reserve the possibility of deciding otherwise in the future, by this very fact he or she would not be giving totally." (Familiaris Consortio, 11)

_____
_____
_____
_____

- If you are married, consider how you use your sexuality in your marriage. Do you truly give a total gift of yourself to your spouse, physically, emotionally, and spiritually? Is your sexual relationship with your spouse an expression of personal trust, intimacy, and union, or more about use, gratification, and pleasure?

- If you are single, and considering marriage, do you respect the gift of your sexuality as a gift that you may someday give to your spouse in the Sacrament of Matrimony?

_____
_____
_____
_____

#2 Do you need any healing or forgiveness in the area of sexuality and purity? Start now by entrusting yourself to the mercy of Christ, and trust that he will give you the grace to love your spouse or possible future spouse with a total and authentic love. Do not be afraid to approach the Sacrament of Reconciliation, where Christ is waiting to forgive, heal, and strengthen you.

CLOSING PRAYER

Love is patient, love is kind.
It is not jealous,
love is not pompous,
it is not inflated,
it is not rude,
it does not seek its own interests,
it is not quick-tempered,
it does not brood over injury,
it does not rejoice over wrongdoing
but rejoices with the truth.
It bears all things,
believes all things,
hopes all things,
endures all things.

—I Corinthians 13:4–7

Photo Credit: Groom carrying bride © popovartem.com/shutterstock.com

Session 8 A LOVE THAT LASTS: PART II

SCRIPTURE VERSE FOR THE WEEK

Here is a verse from the Bible that you can memorize and reflect on this week to help you apply today's session to your daily life:

 Above all hold unfailing your love for one another, since love covers a multitude of sins.

—1 Peter 4:8

DO YOU WANT TO LEARN MORE ABOUT GOD'S PLAN FOR SEXUALITY?

TO ENRICH YOUR CATHOLIC FAITH, VISIT formed.org

Where you'll find helpful videos, audio presentations, ebooks, and feature films from the most trustworthy presenters in the Catholic world.

For Further Reading:

For more in-depth reading about the Church's teaching on sexuality, see the following *Catechism* passages:

- *Sexuality: CCC 2333-2335, 2360–2362*
- *Fecundity of Marriage: CCC 2366*
- *Regulation of Procreation: CCC 2368*

Other Resources:

- **Encyclical Letter, *Humanae Vitae*, by Pope Paul VI**
- **Apostolic Exhortation, *Familiaris Consortio* by Pope St. John Paul II**
- ***Catholic Sexual Ethics: A Summary, Explanation, & Defense*, 3rd Edition by William May, Joseph Boyle, Ronald Lawler**
- ***United States Catholic Catechism for Adults*, Chapter 30 and 33**
- ***Good News about Sex & Marriage: Answers to Your Honest Questions about Catholic Teaching* by Christopher West**

Session 9

CATHOLIC SOCIAL TEACHING

BUILDING A CIVILIZATION OF LOVE

CATHOLIC SOCIAL TEACHING
Building a Civilization of Love

INTRODUCTION

Washing the feet was the kind of task a slave would perform for his master. Yet this is what Jesus did for his disciples the night before he died at the Last Supper. He rose from the table, poured water into a basin, and began to wash his disciples' feet.

Jesus, the Divine Son of God, lowered himself, taking on the role of a slave, to humbly serve his disciples. In doing so, he also wanted to teach them a crucial lesson, a new commandment: "Love one another; even as I have loved you" (John 13:34).

"If I then, your Lord and Teacher, have washed your feet, you ought to wash one another's feet. For I have given you an example, that you also should do as I have done to you" (John 13:14–15).

Ever since the time of the Apostles, Christians have been striving to build a community that is shaped by Christ's command to "love one another" as he loved us. Indeed, already in the early Church, the Gospel message touched on all aspects of human life—marriage and family, education, work, culture, serving the poor, caring for widows, and protecting human life. And it inspired Christians not just to seek their own interests, but to serve each other in all these areas. Through a rich 2,000-year history of striving to live out Christ's call to "wash one another's feet," the Church has also reflected on how to build a just society in which all human beings can flourish. That reflection has been embodied in various principles and guidelines from the Church known as Catholic social teaching.

Session 9 CATHOLIC SOCIAL TEACHING: PART I

THIS SESSION WILL COVER:

- **How the Church's social teaching helps us love one another as Christ loves us**

- **How we are called to imitate Jesus in serving the people right around us: in our families, workplaces, churches, and local communities**

- **How serving and caring for others, especially the poor, is a key characteristic of being a disciple of Christ**

- **How some of the greatest poverty in the world is not material poverty, but a poverty of love or what Pope Francis calls a "poverty of relationships"**

- **The ways that Catholic social teaching affects our lives today and helps us to apply the Gospel to the many social issues we face**

- **The call to responsibility encounter and care for the poor and the most vulnerable around us**

OPENING PRAYER

Father and maker of all,
you adorn all creation
with splendor and beauty,
and fashion human lives
in your image and likeness.
Awaken in every heart
reverence for the work of your hands,
and renew among your people
a readiness to nurture and sustain
your precious gift of life.

Grant this through our Lord
Jesus Christ, your Son,
who lives and reigns with you in
the unity of the Holy Spirit,
one God forever and ever.
Amen.

—Catholic Household Blessings & Prayers at www.usccb.org

> *"To love God and neighbor is not something abstract, but profoundly concrete: it means seeing in every person and face of the Lord to be served, to serve him concretely. And you are, dear brothers and sisters, in the face of Jesus."*
> —Pope Francis

Session 9 CATHOLIC SOCIAL TEACHING: PART I

 ## DISCUSSION QUESTIONS

1. From the very beginning, the Church cared for the poor, the sick, and the abandoned. The Church created the education system and the health care system, and has fed, clothed, and housed more people than any other group or institution in history.

   How does this statement embody Catholic social teaching: "To know Jesus is to want to make him known"?

2. St. Katharine Drexel witnessed with her life that joy is found in what you give and not in what you have. Why do you think true joy is found in generosity and service?

3. How is "encounter" at the heart of social justice?

CALL TO CONVERSION

After spending a few moments in prayer, write down your thoughts and reflections on the following questions:

#1 Reflect on the following quote from Saint Teresa of Calcutta:

"We think sometimes that poverty is only being hungry, naked, and homeless. The poverty of being unwanted, unloved, and uncared for is the greatest poverty. We must start in our own homes to remedy this kind of poverty."

- In what ways does this statement speak to you?

_____
_____
_____
_____
_____
_____

Session 9 CATHOLIC SOCIAL TEACHING: PART I

#2 What poverty do you see around you? Who do you know who is unwanted, unloved, or uncared for? How do you treat the members of your own family? Do you know someone who is going through a very difficult time in their lives?

_____
_____
_____
_____
_____
_____
_____
_____

#3 What is one concrete action you can take this week to begin to meet the needs of those God has placed in your life?

_____
_____
_____
_____
_____
_____
_____
_____

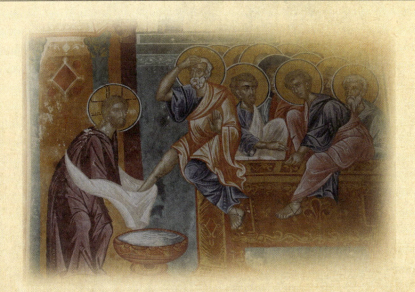

Photo Credit: Washing of Feet at Last Supper © Jorisvo/Shutterstock.com

Session 9 CATHOLIC SOCIAL TEACHING: PART I

CLOSING PRAYER

Come, O Holy Spirit!

Come, open us to the wonder, beauty,
and dignity of the diversity found in each culture,
in each face, and in each experience we have of the other among us.

Come, fill us with generosity as we are challenged to let go and allow others to share with us the goods and beauty of earth.

Come, heal the divisions that keep us from seeing the face of Christ in all men, women, and children.

Come, free us to stand with and for those who must leave their own lands in order to find work, security, and welcome in a new land, one that has enough to share.

Come, bring us understanding, inspiration, wisdom, and the courage needed to embrace change and stay on the journey.

Come, O Holy Spirit,
Show us the way.

—www.usccb.org

Photo Credit: Portrait of a Beautiful Smiling Senior Woman © Kiselev Andrey Valerevich/Shutterstock.com

Session 9 CATHOLIC SOCIAL TEACHING: PART I

SCRIPTURE VERSE FOR THE WEEK

Here is a verse from the Bible that you can memorize and reflect on this week to help you apply today's session to your daily life:

 "Open your mouth, judge justly, defend the needy and the poor!"
—Proverbs 31:9

DO YOU WANT TO KNOW MORE ABOUT BUILDING A CIVILIZATION OF LOVE?

TO ENRICH YOUR CATHOLIC FAITH, VISIT formed.org

Where you'll find helpful videos, audio presentations, ebooks, and feature films from the most trustworthy presenters in the Catholic world.

For Further Reading:

For more in-depth reading about building a civilization of love, see the following *Catechism* passages:

- *Respect for the Human Person: CCC 1928–1933*
- *Solidarity as Part of Social Justice: CCC 1939–1942*
- *Love of Neighbor: CCC 1878*
- *Human Person at the Center of Every Social Organization: CCC 1892*

Other Resources:

- *The United States Catechism for Adults,* **Chapter 24**
- *Compendium of the Social Doctrine of the Church* **(available online from www.vatican.va)**
- *Sharing Catholic Social Teaching: Challenges and Directions* **by United States Conference of Catholic Bishops**
- *Encyclical Letter, Caritas in Veritate* **by Pope Benedict XVI**

Session 9 CATHOLIC SOCIAL TEACHING: PART I
NOTES

Session 10

CATHOLIC SOCIAL TEACHING
PROTECTING THE DIGNITY OF THE HUMAN PERSON

Session 10 CATHOLIC SOCIAL TEACHING: PART II

CATHOLIC SOCIAL TEACHING
Protecting the Dignity of the Human Person

INTRODUCTION

Throughout his public ministry, Jesus went out of his way to associate with the poor, the suffering, and those most vulnerable in society. He visited their homes, came to their assistance, spoke to them as friends, and brought comfort and healing to them. Jesus identified himself so much with the poor that he said the way we treat the poor directly affects our relationship with him.

In a dramatic scene from Matthew 25, Jesus describes how when we go before the judgment seat of God, the chief criterion he will use to evaluate our lives will be how well we served those in need. Did we feed the hungry, give drink to the thirsty, welcome the stranger, clothe the naked, and visit the sick and imprisoned? Those who fail to help the poor and suffering will be cast into eternal punishment, and Jesus explains why: "As you did it not to one of the least of these, you did it not to me" (Matthew 25:45).

This is why Saint Teresa of Calcutta often taught that the Gospel message can be summed up with these five words from Jesus: "You did it to me." In this session, we are going to go deeper into our consideration of Catholic social teaching, exploring how we have a profound responsibility to care for the poor, the sick, the lonely, and the suffering in the world and in our daily lives. And when we do so, we are loving Jesus, who is present in a special way in the poor.

Cover Photo Credit: The good Samaritan by Bassano © Restored Traditions. Used by permission.

Session 10 CATHOLIC SOCIAL TEACHING: PART II

THIS SESSION WILL COVER:

- Why Catholic social teaching contributes to the flourishing of all peoples, not just Catholics
- The difference between rights and responsibilities in society
- Why the essential dignity of each human person is at the heart of Catholic social teaching
- Why abortion and euthanasia are always morally wrong
- What the Church means by a "preferential option for the poor"
- How Catholic social teaching inspires the proper attitude toward earthly possessions and social economic relationships
- What Catholic social teaching tells us about our economic activity and participation in political life

OPENING PRAYER

O God, our Creator,
all life is in your hands
from conception until death.
Help us to cherish our children
and to reverence the awesome privilege
of our share in creation.
May all people live and die in dignity and love.
Bless all those who defend the rights of the unborn,
the handicapped and the aged.
Enlighten and be merciful toward those
who fail to love, and give them peace.
Let freedom be tempered by responsibility,
integrity and morality.

—http://www.catholic.org/prayers/prayer.php?p=228

> *"If you want peace, work for justice!"*
> —Pope Paul VI

Session 10   CATHOLIC SOCIAL TEACHING: PART II

❓ DISCUSSION QUESTIONS

1. What aspects of Catholic social teaching challenge you the most, and why?

2. Reflect on the following quote from St. Basil the Great:

   "The bread you do not use is the bread of the hungry. The garment hanging in your wardrobe is the garment of the person who is naked. The shoes you do not wear are the shoes of the one who is barefoot. The money you keep locked away is the money of the poor. The acts of charity you do not perform are the injustices you commit."

   How does this quote challenge you to be more aware of the needs of the poor? What is something specific you can do in your own life to be a more generous steward of the goods God has entrusted to you, so you can use them not for yourself but to help others?

3. How does the Catholic view of rights and responsibilities differ from the world's view?

CALL TO CONVERSION

In the Gospel of Matthew chapter 25, Jesus tells us that the primary criterion for how God will judge us is how we loved and cared for others. Now imagine that you are going before the judgment seat of God and you see that Jesus is dividing up the people and placing the "sheep" on his right (those who are righteous) and the "goats" on his left (the wicked, who are condemned). You then hear him say to the sheep on the right:

> *"For I was hungry and you gave me food, I was thirsty and you gave me drink, a stranger and you welcomed me, naked and you clothed me, ill and you cared for me, in prison and you visited me…Amen, I say to you, whatever you did for one of these least brothers of mine, you did for me."* (Matthew 25:35-36, 40)

Session 10 CATHOLIC SOCIAL TEACHING: PART II

Then you hear Jesus say to the goats on his left:

"Depart from me, you accursed, into the eternal fire prepared for the devil and his angels. For I was hungry and you gave me no food, I was thirsty and you gave me no drink, a stranger and you gave me no welcome, naked and you gave me no clothing, ill and in prison, and you did not care for me…Amen, I say to you, what you did not do for one of these least ones, you did not do for me." (Matthew 25:41-43, 45)

#1 If you were to go before the judgment seat of God today, which side would you be on?

_____
_____
_____
_____
_____

#2 What changes can you make in your life now to move you even more toward those on the right, who are entering eternal glory?

_____
_____
_____
_____
_____
_____

Photo Credit: The Last Judgment by Cousin © Restored Traditions. Used by permission.

Session 10 CATHOLIC SOCIAL TEACHING: PART II

🕯 CLOSING PRAYER

Lord, you have probed me, you know me:
you know when I sit and stand;
you understand my thoughts from afar.
You sift through my travels and my rest;
with all my ways you are familiar.
Even before a word is on my tongue,
Lord, you know it all…

You formed my inmost being;
you knit me in my mother's womb.
I praise you, because I am wonderfully made;
wonderful are your works!
My very self you know.
My bones are not hidden from you.
When I was being made in secret,
fashioned in the depths of the earth,
your eyes saw me unformed;
in your book all are written down;
my days were shaped, before one came to be.

—Psalm 139

SCRIPTURE VERSE FOR THE WEEK

Here is a verse from the Bible that you can memorize and reflect on this week to help you apply today's session to your daily life:

 "And the king will say to them in reply, 'Amen, I say to you, whatever you did for one of these least brothers of mine, you did for me.'"

—Matthew 25:40

Photo Credit: Close-up of Baby's Hands and Feet Collage © GTeam/Shutterstock.com

Session 10 CATHOLIC SOCIAL TEACHING: PART II

DO YOU WANT TO LEARN MORE ABOUT PROTECTING THE DIGNITY OF THE HUMAN PERSON?

TO ENRICH YOUR CATHOLIC FAITH, VISIT formed.org

Where you'll find helpful videos, audio presentations, ebooks, and feature films from the most trustworthy presenters in the Catholic world.

For Further Reading:

For more in-depth reading about Catholic life and dignity of the human person see the following *Catechism* passages:

- *Human Rights: CCC 1928*
- *Preferential Option for the Poor: CCC 1932*
- *Dignity of Human Life: CCC 2258*
- *Opposition to Abortion: CCC 2270–2275*

Other Resources:

- *United States Catholic Catechism for Adults,* Chapters 24, 28–29, 31–32, 34
- *Compendium of the Social Doctrine of the Church* (available online from www.vatican.va)
- *Sharing Catholic Social Teaching: Challenges and Directions* by United States Conference of Catholic Bishops
- Encyclical Letters, *Laborem Exercens* and *Centesimus Annus* by Pope St. John Paul II
- Encyclical Letter, *Caritas in Veritate* by Pope Benedict XVI

It's not about what it is.
It's about *Who* it is.

Prepare yourself and your family to receive Jesus in the Eucharist as never before with *Presence: The Mystery of the Eucharist*. World-renowned Catholic presenters unveil the truth and beauty behind the "source and summit" of the Christian life, from its origins in Sacred Scripture, to its profound role in the life of the Church and its members.

Learn more at AugustineInstitute.org/Presence

AUGUSTINE INSTITUTE

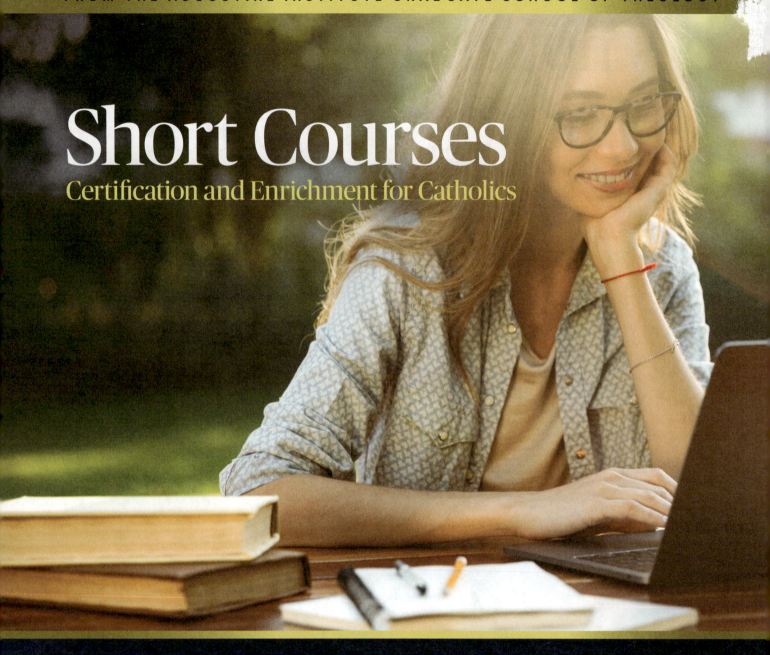

FROM THE AUGUSTINE INSTITUTE GRADUATE SCHOOL OF THEOLOGY

Short Courses
Certification and Enrichment for Catholics

Study Catholic theology online. Develop a deeper understanding of your Catholic Faith with engaging curriculum designed and taught by the Augustine Institute faculty. Earn your certificate in Catholic Theology at the conclusion of the nine-course core curriculum. Each Short Course includes

- Three hours of high-quality video instruction
- Detailed companion presentation slides
- Reading assignments that are modest in length but generous in depth and beauty
- Quizzes to guide your learning
- Related resources: books, video, audio, and more

Learn more at
AugustineInstitute.org/ShortCourses